ISBN: 978-1-62676-634-1

D1810060

Maria Simon is the founder of Eco Heroes, where she helps schools reduce their single-use products waste by helping students realize that their individual action can make a difference in the Planet. She has been awarded "Patron of the Planet" at the Green School Conference during the Climate Week in NYC 2019. She is the mother of Christian [5] and Samuel [4] who inspired her fight against Climate Change in her own way. Maria believes that the only way to change the world is by educating children from a very young age, so they can be one day responsible adults who make sustainable decisions. If you want to learn more about Eco Heroes go to www.ecoheroeskids.com

To Christian, Samuel, Judith, Sofia and Julen. My love for you inspired my personal fight against climate change.

To every child out there reading these words. My faith in you inspired this book!

"You deserve to live on an environmentally safe Planet"

Reading instructions:

This illustrated story shows us how we can come together to save our planet. Being eco-friendly and learning about climate change are part of the steps to securing a future for our children. People of all ages can read this book, and for those young readers, read alongside your parents. Ask them questions! The more you know, the more power you'll have to make a greener, safer world.

By the end of this book you will get REAL SUPERPOWERS, remember that while you are reading the story!

This book belongs to

_____

Sarah sat on her sofa, reading a book about keeping the Earth safe. She turned the pages eagerly, waiting to see how she could reduce her footprint.

"What's that?".

Sarah jumped, startled, turning to see her little brother, Noah pointing out the window. He wore a blue and red superhero costume.

"*Oh, what is it, Noah?*" she said. Sarah crossed the room to see.

Through the window, she saw a big garbage truck outside. Two big forks slid into the grooves of a trash bin. It lifted the bin into the air and dumped all the garbage into the back of the truck, fumes spewing out its tailpipe.

"*Where does all the trash go, Sarah?*" Noah asked.

"Well," said Sarah, "that's one of the reasons the planet is so sick, Noah. We generate too much trash, because we use way too many **single-use** products."

Noah wrinkled his brow and turned to Sarah. "Single-use? What do you mean?"

"Put your shoes on, Noah," said Sarah. "We're going for a walk, and you'll get all the answers you need."

Soon, Sarah and Noah were outside, under the sunshine, walking along.

"See that boy over there, ready to eat his sandwich?" Sarah asked.

Across the street, at a park bench, a boy pulled a sandwich from a plastic bag.

"Yes," said Noah, *"I see him. What's wrong? He's just eating, Sarah."*

Sarah shook her head. "Look closer, Noah. That plastic bag is made from toxic materials, which are nearly unbreakable. That means that even when we use only one, it all adds up.

"Oh," said Noah. "You mean, thousands of plastic bags just sit there, taking up space?"

Sarah replied, *"Yes, plastic bags and all other plastic products we can't put in recycling bins. The place they sit forever are called landfills."*

"And these *landfills,*" Sarah continued, "*can be toxic for us, animals, and the environment.*"

Sarah and Noah kept walking.

They passed a trash can, and Sarah pointed. "*Look, see the plastic dishes, spoons, cups, and toys? People throw these away, but like the plastic bag, they all end up in landfills. Sometimes, landfills get so big, people must burn the trash to reduce the space. This creates **toxic smoke**, and it's not good for the planet either.*"

Noah peeked inside. "*Oh, gross, look at the yogurt inside that cup!*"

He pulled away, plugging his nose and giggling.

Sarah smiled, but she tried to hide it. "*Noah, it's not a laughing matter!*"

He pulled out her smartphone and flipped to a picture of a yogurt cup. *"This was found not too long ago on a beach. Do you see the date on it? 1976! That's over forty years ago, Noah, and it's still like new. It's been floating in the ocean all these years."*

"That's impossible," said Noah, putting his hands on his hips. *"How'd the cup get there?"*

"Perhaps," said Sarah, "someone with the yogurt cup didn't put it in the **recycling bin**. They thought it was trash, so they threw it in with the rest. The garbage truck picked it up, brought it to the **landfill**, and then with rain and time, it found its way to the river."

Sarah and Noah kept walking through the beach.

"And eventually, that yogurt cup went to the ocean!" said Noah. "I understand now."

"Yes, but that's not even the worst part!" Sarah said.

Noah's eyes grew wide. "What? That's not the worst?"

"*Come, follow me, Noah,*" said Sarah.

Together, they walked along the sandy beach to the shore. There, gently rolling waves broke against the sand and rocks.

"*See, out there? There are dolphins, sea lions, fish, and more animals who live in the ocean.*"

Noah waved his arms. "*I love dolphins, Sarah!*"

"Well, the big problem," said Sarah, "is that after so many years, plastic starts breaking up into tiny pieces. This process is called **decomposing**. The poor sea animals confuse the plastic with food and eat it."

"You can't eat plastic!" Noah said.

"Of course, not, so they will get sick...and even die."

"Oh, that's awful, Sarah."

Sarah said, "*Well, if fish eat plastic and we eat fish, we are eating plastic, too!*"

"*Oh no,*" said Noah. "*You mean, we're eating the same trash we throw out?*"

"*That's right,*" Sarah said. "*We are eating our own trash. Look, Noah, I read a study saying that a quarter of all fish in the supermarket contains plastic.*"

Noah spit. "*Yuck, Sarah! That's so gross, I don't want to eat plastic.*"

Sarah smiled, putting an arm around Noah. *"Neither do I! Nobody should have to eat plastic."*

"More people need to recycle, Sarah."

Sarah said, "Recycling is not enough, Noah. **Not all plastics are recyclable**, did you know that?"

Noah shook his head. *"I thought they all were."*

"Oh no, even though people put all plastics into recycling bins, some cannot be recycled."

Scratching his head, Noah said, "Well, how do you know what plastic is recyclable then?"

"That's not so easy!" Sarah said. "But it's not impossible. A way to find out if the plastic is recyclable is by paying attention to the recycle symbol printed on it. Look at this water bottle I found at our school's recycling bin."

Sarah handed Noah a plastic water bottle.

"Oh yeah! There's a little #1 sign on it."

"You got it, Noah. Most people believe that means the product is recyclable, but that symbol tells us what kind of plastic it's made of. So, by learning those numbers, you can learn what kind of plastic should go in your recycle bin."

"Wow!" Noah said brightly. "I didn't know that. Awesome."

"But here is the problem Noah, even if everyone recycles properly, recycling is a process that **pollutes**," Sarah said.

"Pollutes? What's that?"

"Pollutes means you're making pollution, which is **harmful to the planet**. Like the plastic and the smoke that results from burning it, Noah."

Sarah took Noah's hand, and they walked up the path to the road. "See that garbage truck over there, Noah?"

"Yes, I see it."

"That truck has so much smoke coming out of its tailpipe. Just like when people burn the trash to reduce space from **landfills**, that smoke is bad for the planet, too. And when **recycling factories** recycle, there is more smoke like that. All that smoke is **pollution**."

Noah shook his head.
"*It's too much!*"

Noah sat down on the sand, lowering his head onto his hands.

"*Sarah, we're going to have to eat plastic forever!*"

"*No, there's a solution, Noah.*"

Sarah sat down beside her little brother. *"We can stop using plastics altogether. Especially those plastics that we use only one time. Do you remember what we call products we only use once?"*

Noah scratched his head. *"Single-use products? Like sandwich bags?"*

"That's right," Sarah smiled. "Plastic wrap, straws, spoons, bags. All those things. We need to use **reusable products** like mom does."

"And that way, we can reduce the amount of trash we're throwing out. Instead, we can use these items over and over again," Noah said brightly.

"Why can't everyone use reusable products?"

"Some people don't know how big the problem is, Noah, or that they are eating plastic."

"We need to spread the word, Sarah!"

Sarah smiled and hugged Noah.

Noah stood up in his superhero costume, looking at the sparkling ocean and said: "*Sarah, everyone needs to know that we're actually eating plastic!*"

Sarah smiled. "*I think someone found A REAL superpower!*"

"*Look, Sarah, it's our neighbor, Jack,*" Noah shouted. "*Jack! I need to tell you something... you're eating plastic, and you don't even know it.*"

Sarah smiled, running after Noah, ready to spread the word of reducing and finally ending the use of plastics.

TO BE CONTINUED...

Now you've learned how we are eating plastic. And not only us, but the animals, too!

You have, right now, the most incredible superpower: **the power of knowledge.**

You are on a mission to save the world from plastic!

One way you can begin is to help others discover their own superpowers by sharing this book!

WHAT DID YOU LEARN?

COMPLETE THE ACTIVITIES TO SHOW EVERYTHING YOU LEARNED WITH THIS STORY!

1) MATCH THE WORDS WITH THE PICTURES!

LANDFILL

A)

POLLUTION

B)

SINGLE-USE PRODUCTS

C)

DECOMPOSE

D)

2) DRAW THESE EVENTS AND PUT THEM IN ORDER TO SHOW HOW WE END UP EATING PLASTIC!

NUMBER _____: THE FISH CONFUSE PLASTIC WITH FOOD

NUMBER _____: WE BUY FISH IN THE SUPERMARKET

NUMBER _____: OUR TRASH GOES TO THE OCEAN

3) ANSWER THE QUESTIONS ABOUT POLLUTION!

A) WHERE DOES THE TRASH WE THROW OUT GO?
COLOR THE CORRECT ANSWERS.

CLOTHES
LANDFILLS
OCEAN
ANIMALS
CLOUDS

B) WHAT ARE THE DIFFERENT TYPES OF POLLUTION MENTIONED IN THE STORY?
NAME THE IMAGES.

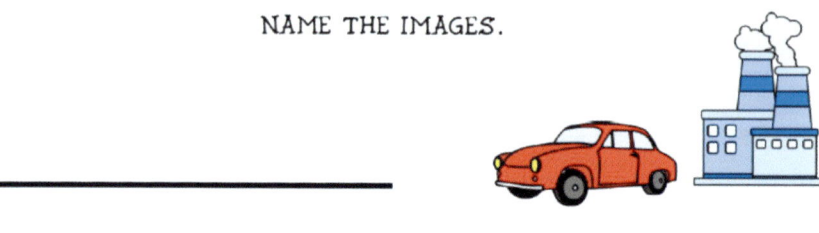

_____

_____

_____

4) WHAT CAN YOU DO TO REDUCE SINGLE-USE PRODUCTS WASTE?

_____

_____

_____

5) CIRCLE THE CORRECT ANSWER!

WHAT PART OF THE STORY SHOWS PLASTIC TAKES A LONG TIME TO DECOMPOSE?

WHEN SARAH TELLS NOAH ABOUT A YOGURT CUP IN THE SHORE

WHEN NOAH SEES A BOY EATING A SANDWICH WITH A PLASTIC BAG

WHEN NOAH AND SARAH SEE THE SMOKE FROM A TRUCK

DO YOU THINK WHAT SARAH TELLS NOAH IS TRUE?

_____

EXTRA ACTIVITIES
NUMBER 6 & 7

6) COMPLETE THE QUIZ!

1) HOW DO YOU USUALLY GET TO SCHOOL?

A) RIDE WITH PARENTS — 2 POINTS
B) RIDE THE BUS — 1 POINTS
C) WALK, RIDE A BICYCLE — 0 POINTS

2) DO YOU TAKE MORE SHOWERS OR BATHS?

A) SHOWERS — 0 POINTS
B) BATHS — 1 POINTS

3) HOW OFTEN DO YOU TURN OFF THE WATER WHEN YOU BRUSH YOUR TEETH?

A) NEVER — 2 POINTS
B) SOMETIMES — 1 POINT
C) ALWAYS — 0 POINTS

4) HOW OFTEN DO YOU AND YOUR FAMILY RECYCLE AT HOME?

A) NEVER — 2 POINTS
B) SOMETIMES — 1 POINT
C) ALWAYS — 0 POINTS

5) DO YOU PACK YOUR LUNCHBOX USING REUSABLE PRODUCTS?

A) YES — 0 POINTS
B) NO — 1 POINTS

NOW ADD YOUR SCORE!

HOW DID YOU DO? _____ POINTS

THE LOWER YOUR SCORE, THE MORE
ENVIRONMENTALLY FRIENDLY YOU ARE ACTING!

7) WHAT TYPES OF PLASTIC CAN YOU RECYCLE?
JUST LOOK AT THE SPI CODES, LIKE SARAH EXPLAINED TO NOAH IN THE STORY!

EASY TO RECYCLE!
YOU CAN PUT IT IN YOUR RECYCLING BIN!
👍 1 2

MORE DIFFICULT TO RECYCLE
FIND OUT IF YOU CAN PUT IT IN YOUR RECYCLING BIN!
👉 4 5

VERY HARD TO RECYCLE
YOU CAN'T PUT IT IN YOUR RECYCLING BIN. FIND A SPECIAL CURBSIDE PROGRAM!
👎 3 6 7

AS AN ECO-HERO YOU WOULD WANT TO USE ONLY PRODUCTS THAT FOR SURE ARE GOING TO GET RECYCLED.

WHAT PRODUCTS' SPI WOULD YOU USE? _____

NOW YOU CAN BE A REAL HERO AND SAVE THE WORLD FROM SINGLE-USE PRODUCTS WASTE!

CHECK YOUR ANSWERS AT HTTPS://ECOHEROESKIDS.COM/PAGES/YOU-ARE-EATING-PLASTIC

Eco Heroes' Fundraising program for schools

The average-size elementary school in the US produces 18,760 pounds of lunch waste per school year.

MORE THAN 50% OF THAT WASTE COMES FROM PLASTIC MATERIALS!

Share these numbers with your school and suggest that they participate in an Eco Heroes' fundraising programs for schools, where they will be able to raise money for the school or organization they choose while reducing the amount of waste "saving the world from single-use products waste".

Book Fundraising:

Invite students in your school to purchase this book where they will get the power of knowledge needed to save the world from single-use products waste.

Products Fundraising:

Invite students' families to pack single-use products in their snacks and lunch box. This's the best way to reduce the amount of waste we are putting in landfills and MAKE A CHANGE IN THE WORLD! Eco Heroes provides catalogs to students' families.

Win an Eco Hero award if your school reduces more than 30% of their waste.

Participation is simple, just go to www.ecoheroeskids.com and register your school!

Printed in Poland
by Amazon Fulfillment
Poland Sp. z o.o., Wrocław